A Concise

History of Medicine

By.
Sir. William Osler, M. D. F. R. S.
Regius Professor of Medicine
in the University of Oxford

Published by permission
of the
Encyclopaedia Americana Publishing Co.

The Medical Standard Book Co.
Baltimore, Md.

HISTORY OF MEDICINE.

Within the past three centuries the average working life of English-speaking men has doubled. A few lived as long as now, and some strong or favored ones had efficient working powers as long; but the common life was worn out in what is now middle age. In Shapespeare's time the 50's were venerable: "Old John of Gaunt, time-honored Lancaster," was 58 when supposedly so addressed; and Admiral Coligny, murdered at 53, is described by his contemporary biographer as a very old man. Now, when we hear of a death in the 60's, we instinctively feel it an untimely cutting off, in what should be still fresh and vigorous age, and even at 80 it seems but just fair ripeness for the sickle. The three factors which have wrought this change are advanced physical comfort, medicine and its handmaid hygiene, and surgery. And in the mitigation of the frightful mass of actual pain, of physical torment which has racked every age down to the present, and which has scarcely even been alleviated till the past century, medicine stands incomparably first.

Some good foundations have been laid, it is true, in the century previous, and men were at work in the true scientific spirit. Great masters had stimulated their successors to study in the essential preliminary subjects, the constitution and functions of the body. The mighty Boerhaave of Holland (1668-1738) had revolutionized clinical observation; Morgagni of Italy (1682-1771) had "introduced anatomical thinking into medicine" (Virchow), and had done something, the same service for pathology which Haller of Germany (1708-77) did a generation later for physiology; while John Hunter (1728-93) had not only introduced capital improvements into operative surgery, but had set the pace in research into anatomical and physiological problems. But the influence of old theories, founded on guesses and imperfectly interpreted observation, still lay heavy on the body of practitioners. The chief general theories in the 18th century were those of William Cullen (1710-90) and his pupil and assistant, John Brown (1736-88), of the University of Edinburgh; the former— a great advance on the older theory of "humors," and on the right track—made the nervous system the seat of diseases; the latter divided all diseases into two classes—the sthenic, resulting from overexcitation and treated by depletion, and the asthenic, resulting from under-excitation and treated by stimulation. On the Continent, Hahnemann (1755-1843), his great theory propounded at Leipsic (1796-1810), soon after took adverse ground in his "homeopathy—a very different thing from what later passed under the name, though the latter retained the underlying basis. Besides his "law of similars" which Hippocrates had formulated before him, he rejected theory utterly, declaring that it was impossible to know anything about pathological changes out of sight; that we can only know symptoms, and if those are removed it indicates of necessity that the disease which produced them must be gone, also. He also alleged that the fact of a given dose causing certain symptoms in a healthy person was obvious proof that it must be too large for a sick one; further, that to possess healing power the dose must be too small for recognition by the senses or chemical analysis; and that trituration, or dilution and shaking of minute doses caused molecular changes which infinitely increased their power—"dynamization," he termed it. The exaggeration of symptomatics and empirics was a reaction against the current reliance on unbased theories; the paradox of infinitesimal doses, against the monstrous boluses and draughts with which patients were often gravely injured; there was usefulness in both reactions, but he went so far as to declare that a child could be cured while asleep by holding the pellets near it.

But the reign both of guesswork theorizing and of groping empirics, as exclusive methods, was coming to an end, and the first great blow was delivered in the first year of the century. France now came to the front where other countries had thronged. Bichat, a genius, who wore himself out at 31, as did Clifford at 34, published the year before his death (1801) a work on general anatomy, in which he remade the entire science by showing that the different organs have membranes and tissues in common, and, therefore, that the seat of disease was in the constituent tissues and not in the organs as such. This not only simplified anatomy and physiology in much the same way that the alphabet simplified hieroglyphics, but threw the investigation of pathological changes into an entirely new channel. Parallel with this work, the followers in the footsteps of

Morgagni were carrying on his work in studying morbid anatomy, the appearances of diseased organs; this, too, was remodeled on Bichat's discoveries. In 1808 and 1816 Broussais of Paris (1772-1838) published valuable works whose theory is merely the sthenic and asthenic idea of Brown, but which led to renewed research in pathological anatomy and local ailments. Percussion had been devised by Auenbrugger of Vienna (1722-1809) in 1761, and Corvisart of Paris (1755-1821) revived it; but a greater effect was created by the introduction of auscultation (1816-19) by the Breton Laennec (1781-1826) at Paris, where he was Corvisart's pupil. He invented the stethoscope to diagnose diseases of the lungs, heart and abdominal organs, by means of alteration in the normal sounds of their action; and his own use of it, and observations on the diseases of these organs, were the greatest advance made in clinics since Boerhaave, and may be said to have founded modern clinical science. In 1827, Richard Bright at London (1789-1858) first published his recognition of the true nature of the kidney disease since called by his name, and of the general characteristics of renal complaints, the foundation of our knowledge of them.

A special branch of investigation and analysis in the first half of the century was in discriminating the continued fevers; one of the most active and anxious battle-grounds for practitioners and theorists since modern medicine took its rise, though eruptive and malarial fevers were well differentiated. The first to be discriminated was typhoid, by Louis of Paris (1787-1872). His American pupils, W. W. Gerhard (1809-72- and Alfred Stille (1803), with C. W. Pennock (1799-1867), all of Philadelphia, and George B. Shattuck, of Boston, proved that typhoid and typhus, theretofore loosely classed together, were independent diseases, though generated by similar causes. This was confirmed by the work of A. P. Stewart at Glasgow and Sir William Jenner at London. Dengue or break-bone fever, yellow and relapsing fevers, and their kind, were carefully studied. Among the other names associated with this labor are R. J. Graves (1797-1853) and William Stokes (1804-78) of Dublin, George Budd (1808-82) of London, and Daniel Drake (1785-1852), S. H. Dickson (1798-1872), and Austin Flint (1812-86) in America. This work was soundly based by 1860 in regard to fever clinics.

Development in the United States.— When the 19th century opened there were only three medical schools in the United States, and only two of importance— those connected with Harvard College and the University of Pennsylvania—and only two general hospitals. Medical education was somewhat on a footing with divinity education; physicians took apprentices for some years, and clergymen took private pupils in divinity. Those who wished and could afford a more systematic medical education went to London or Edinburgh. The literature of the profession was English and (translated) French almost wholly; Rush and a few others had published books, but not of moment, and there were only two or three medical journals. There were but two medical libraries, except in private hands—those at the New York and the Pennsylvania Hospitals. The physicians of most reputation were Benjamin Rush and Philip S. Physick, of Philadelphia; David Hosack and Samuel L. Mitchill, of New York, and James Jackson and John C. Warren, of Boston. The smaller places did not lack for able men, though of less wide-spread repute, such as Daniel Drake, of Cincinnati, and Nathan Smith, founder of the medical schools both of Dartmouth and of Yale. But the great repute of the French medical investigators in the first quarter of the century—Bichat, Corvisart, Laennec, Louis, etc.—

took an increasing number of American
students there, and the new spirit they
brought back revolutionized American
practice for a time. The enormous increase in American population, however,
enlarged the demand upon its stock of
medical knowledge far faster than that
could be legitimately developed; educated
physicians could not be turned out so
fast as the thronging populace needed
them, and it was the golden age of the
half-educated. Perhaps, too, the masses
had the same ideas of the needlessness
of training in medicine as in public life.
The machinery was multiplied indefi-
nitely, and the product turned out de-
preciated in proportion. Up to about
1870 the medical schools sprung up every-
where, both public and private, and their
competition for pupils degraded the standard very low indeed. Diplomas were given
for two years' work, and short sessions at
that; and the instructors were sometimes
as incapable of giving competent education as the authorities were unwilling to

enforce severe study or careful experiment.   The first place to exact a new and much higher standard was Harvard, about 1870.   The rapidity with which the rest of the country, in the better institutions, followed its lead showed that there was a large instructed upper class which appreciated the need of thorough education in this as in other departments of knowledge, and understood that medicine was a great science as well as a delicate craft.   As always, the rich were glad to give when they knew where to give intelligently, and endowed generously both study laboratories and general and special hospitals.   It would be a grateful task to enumerate these, did space permit; here can be mentioned only such names as Pierpont Morgan and Andrew Carnegie, Johns Hopkins and Vanderbilt, Sims, Strathcona, Mount-Stephen, Payne and Lane.

Methods of Investigation.—The last century, of course, did not invent experiment in medicine or physiology; the method was recognized by the great Greek and Latin physicians, used by the two great Bacons, Roger and Francis, fully developed by Harvey, and utilized with superb skill by Hunter. But though these great men did not lack sound ideas, they lacked tools and the mass of laboratory facilities gradually built up in our age. The research laboratory is the development of the 19th century, and well along toward the middle of it. The workers in it experiment along three main lines —the condition and functions of the organs in a state of health; the nature of the functional changes produced by disease, and the causes of the changes; and the prophylactic or curative agencies which can neutralize the disturbing agents. The results of these studies have created a new knowledge, which is to that of even 1800 like the relation of an adult to a baby. The physiological and pathological revelations have not merely left the knowledge accumulated in the previous centuries possessed of a merely archeological interest, but they have weaned us from the sway of any authority whatever; recognizing that even the seemingly soundest conclusions of the present are but working hypotheses, which may have to be abandoned at any time on fresh evidence—the true scientific spirit. No part of life has been left as it was, the digestive and assimilative, circulatory, respiratory and excretory, reproductive and directive functions have all been illuminated by a flood of light. Especially has this been wonderful in the study of the brain, whose functions not only are so intangible and elusive, but apparently so impossible of experimentation without destroying the subject of experiment. Not only have we penetrated deep into the secrets of the paths and operations of sensory and motor impulses, the localization of functions, and the mechanical implements of thought and memory, but we have been enabled to apply with great success a number of curative measures not before dreamed of, or even if so, not deemed possible of use.

Another marked feature of the age is the development of specialism, in which we have to set off a lack of co-ordination and breadth of knowledge or judgment against an extension of knowledge not possible by any other method. Scientifically no other means has been so potent in extending and deepening the realm of demonstrated fact. Practically no other has been so effective in developing curative processes. This specialism must not be confounded with that of the "lung doctors" and "fever doctors" of former days, mere guesswork empiricism of uneducated practitioners; it rests on a basis of competent general medical knowledge and thorough education in the specialty besides. The physicians who give their time and thought to one limited field— diseases of women, of children, of eyes and ears, of throat, of teeth, of the brain, or who, though less eclusively, choose diseases of the heart or the liver or other organs for their preferred field—have won for the profession some of its most signal triumphs. American physicians especially have stood at the very head of those who have perfected dentistry and opthalmology, as well as gynaecology or diseases of women. In this branch the blessings they have conferred not only on women in ordinary disease, but on both them, their male relatives, and their children, by the saving of life and health, in the special diseases of the sex, cannot be estimated.

One of the finest branches of this specializing is that of alienism, and the change in the mental attitude of the public toward it in consequence of that study has been most remarkable and gratifying. From a matter of derision, as it was largely in the Middle Ages, or ineffectual commiseration as an act of God, or mere terror and aversion, it has come to be sympathetically studied, often relieved, and always recognized as a mere functional disease. Starting from the labors of our own Rush, of the English Tuke, of the German Jacobi and Hasse, and the French Pinel and Esquirol, this reform has built up a body of physicians in every civilized country not only to study mental aberration scientifically, but to introduce humane and rational methods into its care and cure. America is not behind any other in the treatment of the insane; but the curse of so many good causes in America—politics—is a blight upon this science still in too many States.

Prophylactics. — "Prevention is better than cure" has reached its most brilliant exemplification in the 19th century. It is true that nations far back in antiquity have grasped some of the chief conditions under which diseases most prevail, and have even carried systems of public hygiene much farther than even yet we have reattained to. The law of Moses furnishes a remarkable example, in its

insistence on cleanliness, isolation and
diet; the Greeks systematized diet and
exercise and general physical training
thoroughly, their ideal being "the fair
mind in the fair body" (and had discovered that professional athletes do not
make good soldiers, from lack of endur-
ance); the Romans and Greeks made the
bath almost a fetish, far beyond even the
English, and the public benefactor of the
day gave his city baths, not libraries. But
modern science goes much farther; it dis-
cerns the causes which create the disease
itself, and removes or neutralizes them.
In the 18th century some light had been
thrown on this: Howard had seen that
typhus was in direct ratio to the crowded
condition of jails, Captain Cook and Sir
Gilbert Blaine had perceived and removed
the conditions that generate scurvy. Jenner had gone still farther and anticipated
the methods of modern preventive medicine by vaccination. But all these could
only be feeble and groping attempts until
there was a scientific basis for them. This

was furnished by bacteriology, and a few
words upon that are needed to make later
explanations intelligible.

THE BACTERIOLOGICAL BASIS OF
PREVENTIVE MEDICINE.

The ancients speculated with great
eagerness and sometimes acuteness on the
origin of life, and had guessed that disease and living germs were in some way
related; and the relation of disease and
putrefaction was not doubted. As soon
as the first weak crude microscope was
invented, it was used to investigate the
organisms of decay. The Jesuit Kircher
in 1671 examined the "minute worms" in
putrid milk and cheese and meat; in 1675
a Dutch merchant named Leeuwenhoek
improved his lenses and studied the "ani-
malcula" in rainwater, saliva, intestinal
fluids, and putrid substances; and the
physicians of his day were quick to sus-
pect and suggest that these organisms
might be the cause of all diseases. In

1762 the Viennese Pleincz, who had studied fluids in all conditions, gave his firm adhesion to this belief. But this was not the whole; whence came these organisms—were they self-generated, or simply transmitted from other bodies and multiplied? Despite even the microscope, the theory of spontaneous generation maintained itself tenaciously far past the middle of the century. A distinguished chemist maintained as the result of careful experiment that germs were so generated, and even the proof that the organisms were forms already existent did not convince him or his followers. It was reserved for Pasteur in 1861, and finally (with Koch and Cohn) in 1876, to crush this theory forever. Following quickly on the first came the discovery of the anthrax germ by Pollender and Davaine in 1863; shortly afterward Lister's epoch-making researches into wound infection, making possible the triumphs of antiseptic surgery; then swiftly followed the isolation of the germs of relapsing fever, lep-

rosy and typhoid. But towering above
all, from the enormous difficulties overcome, were Robert Koch's isolations of
the tuberculosis germ in 1882, and of
that of Asiatic cholera in 1884. Thence on
a crowd of discoveries of the germs of
other diseases have left but few—unfor-
tunately, some of the worst—unrevealed,
diseases of animals and insects having
been investigated as well as those of men.

Thus much for the history of discovery;
but what are these germs? The popular
mind is very confused on the subject.
Bacteria are generally thought of as a
sort of worm. In fact, they are not mem-
bers of the animal, but the vegetable king-
dom; the smallest organisms known. They
are protoplasm, a jelly-like substance, en-
closed in a hard membrane exactly like
wood fibre. They are classified by shape
in three groups: Cocci (spherical), bacilli
(rod-like), and spirilla (corkscrew or un-
dulatory shape). The cocci are found in
pairs, fours, clusters or chains; they in-

clude the smallest known organisms, some
of them being as small as 1/150,000 of an
inch in diameter. The bacilli are larger,
but vary much, from 1/25,000 to 1/4,000
of an inch inlength, and 1/125,000 to
1/16,000 in diameter; some of them have
organs of locomotion, called flagella. The
spirilla are longest of all, sometimes 1/600
of an inch. They all increase either by
fission into two, or by developing a spore
or seed. Their rate of multiplication does
not seem rapid, but that is because we for-
get our old arithmetical "catches." A
bacterium dividing each hour, and each
division thus dividing, would obviously
have increased to 8,388,608 in 24 hours,
and in three days to a number beyond
all verbal expression, weighing nearly
7,500 tons. Of course, this is a reductio
ad absurdum, as the body they feed on
would be exhausted early in the series;
but outside of starvation nature has other
ways of arresting their multiplication.

Before discussing this point, let us look
at the nature of bacteria as a whole. It

is a misapprehension to think of them simply as a principle of disease and death. They are a universal principle of life as well, and the few species which cause harm are lost in the myriads which do good. But for them organic existence would perish; it has been suggested that the first organic things on earth were bacteria—organisms needing only nitrogen for support—and life means their multiplication. They abound in air and water, in the soil to nine feet deep or so, and in the outsides and insides of all organisms; but naturally their number varies with the conditions for sustaining existence, and there are none at extreme altitudes or in glacier ice, and few in the polar regions or the deep seas. Those conditions are (1) moisture, without, which all die; (2) air, as to which there are three classes—aerobes, which must have it; anaerobes, which must not have it, and facultative anaerobes, which care nothing either way; (3) food, which must be living tissues for a few, may be dead ones for most, and can be mineral salts or atmospheric nitrogen for some; (4) temperature, which has for possibilities of their multiplication, though not of their life, extremes of 32 and 170° F.; for an average most favorable tract 60 to 104°, and for disease germs (as evolution would imply) is most favorable 98.4°, or blood heat; (5) light, of which direct sunlight is death to all, and common daylight of no importance either way to most.

Their enormous number gives them a power of accomplishment seemingly almost miraculous, and certainly far superhuman. The quality of farm products and dairy products, of fatted stock or wool, of hides or horn, and many other familiar articles, is due to them; and they are the scavengers of our water supply from pollution, as well as some of them deriving powers for harm from it. Still more to our surprise, peas and beans certainly, and all plants probably, gain their life from the soil through the medium of bacteria which live in their roots, decompose nitrogenous minerals and feed on atmospheric nitrogen also, turning both kinds over to the plant for its nourishment.

Hence the processes of health and disease alike are functions of bacteria. What medical science has specially to do is to trace the progress and manifestations of that spread of harmful bacteria commonly called "infection," and the methods by which the system's natural tendency to starve or poison them can be reinforced. Before entering upon the phases of prevention and cure, we must indicate briefly how they obtain entrance, how they produce their effects, and what is the reaction of the body thereupon.

The first is naturally limited in variety; they enter by being injected from the bites of animals or insects, from wounds or abrasions, from inhaling infected air, from eating or drinking substances containing them. Specific cases will be considered later. The action of the microbes is by generating a set of poisons known as toxins, which produce either languor, loss of appetite, and vague general discomfort, or more active pains, headaches, fevers, inflammations of the tissues, perhaps entire stupor. The action of the body is complex and difficult, and not thoroughly worked out; but some things are known. The normal blood and tissues have a germicidal power, varying in different bodies even of full health, and varying still more as to specific germs, each body having its own set of germs to which it is congenial or maleficent. The struggle of the body against their multiplication, dependent on this unfavorableness of soil for their propagation, is called "general resistance," and on its strength depends the immunity against ordinary disease; and the secret of inoculation is, that if the soil favorable to the propagation of a specific bacterium is eaten up, it is usually very slow in fresh growth. The disease microbe gains no lodgment because there is nothing to live on. But in addition to this passive resistance, an active one is carried on by the white cells or "leucocytes"—the wandering cells, and those of the tissues chiefly invaded, as well as those of the spleen and lymphatic glands; these and others seem to work among the toxins and produce a change in their chemical constitution, at last elaborating counter-poisons or antitoxins which neutralize the first, and enable the cells to carry on the war against the disease microbes till one or other is overcome; and as said, if there is recovery, a partial or complete immunity is afforded against further ravages of the same class of microbe.

But it is evident that if this process can be shortened and made more certain, so that the antitoxins can perform their work before the disease microbes arrive at all, a great system of prophylactic or preventive medication can be had; and if the antitoxins are used in a case of similar disease, they will strengthen the natural power of the body to develop them, and greatly aid it in throwing off the disease. This is the new system of serum-therapy, begun by Pasteur in 1877, and continued by a set of brilliant experimenters since. The serum of the infected blood is chosen as a medium for injection into the blood of the patient. Pasteur with fowl cholera, Raynaud with cow-pox, Salmon and Smith in this country in 1886 with hog cholera, fully proved the possibility of the treatment, curing animals previously inoculated with the most virulent disease poisons, and rendering healthy animals immune; but these excited but languid interest till Behring's announcement in 1892 of a diphtheria antitoxin, with incontestable proof of its value. Oddly, not only laymen, but physicians in many cases, opposed it; partly from misunderstanding, partly from humanitarianism as involving experiments on animals. Most of its opponents have now been won over, from the crushing

weight of evidence, and the brilliant work
of its supporters. Diphtheria alone has
reduced its mortality one-half since the
introduction of the serum treatment little
more than a decade ago.

To illustrate the general methods of
preparing all the serums for infectious
diseases, that of diphtheria will serve as
a model. The bacilli are cultivated for
eight or ten days in alkaline beef broth,
found to develop a peculiarly virulent
poison under its work; the toxin is then
isolated and its strength precisely estimated, then set aside in sterilized vessels.
A healthy horse, found by experiment the
most suitable animal, has injected under
the skin of its neck or forequarters 20
cubic cm. of toxin and perhaps half that
of antitoxin, three times five days apart;
then it is given heavier and heavier doses
of toxin alone, a week apart, till it can
endure doses speedily fatal at the outset.
After two months it is bled and its serum
tested; if satisfactory, it is dosed as before

for another month, when the maximum quality of serum is usually reached. The animal is then bled sufficiently, the blood being caught in a sterilized vessel and placed in a refrigerator. The coagulation finished, the serum is drawn off from the clot and its strength accurately determined in the laboratory, an antiseptic is added to keep it, and it is bottled for use. Antitoxins for tetanus and snake bite have been similarly prepared, and the present century will see probably every infectious disease and every venom with its bacterial antidote.

SPECIFIC RESULTS OF PREVENTIVE TREATMENT.

An abstract of the work already done in preventive medicine can best be given by a note of the great maladies of men and animals more or less controlled by it, with their bacteria. But it must be noted that of the ones cited, the bacteria of smallpox and hydrophobia (though the former has been almost exterminated by vaccination), as well as scarlet fever and measles, have not yet been isolated. The reason may be excessively small size, since that of cattle pleuro-pneumonia is barely visible under the microscope; or it may be that the organisms are not bacteria, but unknown beings.

The diseases may be classified variously and some admit no special classification, but we will begin with the great scourges past, and which have owed their virulence and destructiveness, though not their direct origin, to filth and overcrowding and general unsanitary conditions.

(1) The Great Plague, or Bubonic Plague. The frightful devastations of this in the past need not be recited; it will be remembered that it was the "Black Death," which swept off from a third to a half the population of Europe in the latter part of the 13th century. Long thought almost extinct, it reappeared with

fearful intensity at Hong-Kong in 1894, spread to India and had several occasions of violent outbreak, raged in Turkey and on some parts of the Mediterranean coast, and in small volume has shown itself in Glasgow, South American ports, New York and San Francisco. But in Western Europe and America it has been easily put down, and serum inoculation has been fairly successful in India. Its bacillus is known to enter the body by wounds of the skin, and very largely by bites of fleas from infected rats.

(2) Asiatic Cholera. This terrible plague, even in the middle of the 19th century, swept away thousands of lives in America; now it has been so thoroughly controlled that it is not feared even to the extent of disturbing commerce when it appears. It originated on the banks of the Ganges in India, where Koch found its spirillum and the means of its spread—almost entirely through drinking infected water, though very slightly by contact—

so little that since 1873 the disease in
Great Britain and the United States has
never got farther than the port of entry.
How thoroughly a city's immunity depends on its water supply is strikingly
shown by the twin city on the Elbe in
1892; Hamburg using the unfiltered river
water, had about 18,000 cases and 8,000
deaths; Altona, with a filtration plant, had
516 cases, largely refugees from Hamburg.

(3) Typhus Fever. It is hard to believe that this was once so steady and
frightful a curse in the West that one in-
vestigator says its history would be that
of Europe. In all the large cities, in
camps and ships, hospitals and jails, it
was almost permanent, and its rate of
mortality appalling. It depended so entirely on filth and over-crowding that
mere city sanitation and cessation of pack-
ing, sewers and a good water supply, have
practically exterminated it except in a
few slums. The rate has been reduced
in England from 1,228 per 1,000,000 in

1838 (typhus and typhoid together, not then discriminated) to 137 typhoid and 3 typhus.

(4) Typhoid Fever. This disease, long identified with typhus, is now not only known to be separate, but dependent on somewhat different generating conditions. It depends not so much on dirt and crowding as on sewer gases and contaminated water and milk. Given pure water and perfect drainage, a city practically has no typhoid, except when its milk supply is drawn from infected sources, as often happens; while seaside resorts are notorious generators of the disease, from the sand-driven wells and the crowded privies draining ino them. The germ was discovered by Eberth in 1880, and called bacillus typhosus. The continued prevalence of the disease in our cities is due partly to the great hardiness of the bacillus, which can exist in the body of a patient long after recovery, and be a means of contamination. The outbreak

in the Spanish-American war seemed due
to overcrowding, but more likely to the
contaminations caused by it, as in the seaside cases. In the country districts there
is no mystery about it; often there is no
rural sanitation, and even the wells are
grossly neglected, sometimes on a slope
below a barn. In the typical example at
Plymouth, Pa. (about 8,000 people), the
evacuations of a typhoid patient were
thrown out during the winter on the
banks of a stream which fed the town
reservoir; the spring thaw carried them
into it, and the own had a typhoid epi-
demic which struck down 1,200 people.
The proper precautions are the use of
boiled water, and of distilled-water ice,
the thorough inspection of dairy sur-
roundings and water sources, and great
care on the part of physicians and nurses
to disinfect discharges, are the true prophylactics.

(5) Diphtheria. This bacillus was discovered in 1883-4 by Klebs and Loeffler,
and has been given their joint names; it

enters either by inhalation or the stomach. The antitoxins thus made possible of preparation have reduced the mortality one-half; the hygienic precautions have greatly reduced the primary prevalence. The latter are isolation and disinfection, watchfulness during convalescence, careful examination of the least throat disorder, and —since the mild and often unsuspected cases where the children go about and to school freely are the worst in spreading disease, because not guarded against— regular inspection of school children's throats. Children's teeth and mouths should also be carefully attended to, and the tonsils removed where tonsilitis is frequent.

(6) Yellow Fever. The germ of this has not yet been isolated. Its dependence on dirt, however, would seem almost as close as typhus, thorough sanitation having practically eradicated it in its favorite tropic home, Havana, and in the Southern cities once ravaged by it. Jamaica has been almost freed from it in the same way.

(7) Smallpox. This once widespread and sometimes destructive scourge, almost more dreaded for life than for death, has been so nearly eradicated by vaccination, and vaccination alone, that the persistence of a strong section of the community opposed to it is one of the strangest of phenomena. The evidence is overwhelming. Wherever smallpox breaks out it is in an unvaccinated district, country, or body of people, and the fatalities are almost all among the unvaccinated and never among the re-vaccinated; where two bodies of men lie side by side under the same conditions, as the French and German armies in 1871, the vaccinated body scarcely suffers, the unvaccinated one is decimated; and in Egypt, where the natives are compulsorily vaccinated and the foreigners escape it, the fatalities are five foreigners to three natives, though the latter are far poorer, worse housed and fed and medically cared for, and would naturally be supposed the chief victims. If all the people of a country

were vaccinated, and re-vaccinated at fair
intervals, the disease would absolutely
disappear, as it has in the German army;
it is the ones who escape vaccination that
maintain its existence. The ravages still
among the unvaccinated French-Cana-
dians are a constant example of what it
has been. For instance, on April 1, 1885,
there was a smallpox death in the Mont-
real Hospital, the Hotel Dieu; the patients who had not had it were sent home;
the disease spread like wildfire, and by
the end of the year 3,164 persons died
of it, the city's business for the winter
was destroyed, and the loss was millions.
It has been proved that not above one in
100 of the vaccinated takes the disease
when exposed, and almost none die; of the
unvaccinated, fully 99 per cent take it and
25 to 30 die. It must be remembered,
however, that there cannot be perfect se-
curity without frequent re-vaccination, as
the power of the cow-pox varies with different persons and is rarely permanent,
sometimes not over a year or two. With

animal lymph there is no danger of the
introduction of other diseases, the fear
of which is made an excuse for refusal.

(8) Tuberculosis (including "consumption" of the lungs), called by Holmes the
"white plague"; the most destructive sin-
gle agency of death, and responsible for
120,000 deaths a year in the United States,
more than all other infectious diseases together, except pneumonia. Formerly be-
lieved hereditary (the truth in a very
slight degree), it is now known to be the
product of a bacillus, isolated by Koch in
1880-2; and the hereditary conditions are
. mainly environment, with some tendency
to anaemia. The communication, though
in a few cases by infected milk, in the
overwhelming mass proceeds by inhalation of the particles of dried sputum from
other consumptives' lungs, blown about
in the dust of streets or houses, or even
wards of hospitals. Naturally, the greatest mortality is in places where free circulation of air is not possible, as jails and

"institutions." Nature seems to have provided for the largest possible distribution of them; one patient not in extremes has been known to give off from two to four thousand millions of germs in 24 hours; they are shaken from handkerchiefs, from the beard or mustache, from the furniture and other things handled oy consumptives, beaten up from contaminated floors. So universally diffused are they that it seems probable there are few persons who have not some tuberculous lesion of some organ, for it is not confined to the lungs. The great weapons against it are, first, maintaining the standard of nutrition and cleanliness as high as possible; with careful protection of the chest; second, the education of the public in the dangers of the dried sputa; third, enforcement of notification and registration of cases; fourth, public sanatoriums for treatment of early cases; fifth, special hospitals for incurables. Immense progress has already been made; the rate in Massachusetts, one of the chief seats of the disease, has fallen from 42 to under $1 per 1,000 since 1853; and in New York, Glasgow, and other great cities the drop has been similar.

(9) Pneumonia. Frankel in 1886 isolated this germ, a coccus growing in pairs and chains and entering by inhalation, and with one-fifth of healthy persons present in the saliva. This is almost the one disease which has not diminished under medical and hygienic science, and has apparently increased, ranking next to consumption in deadliness. It is especially a disease of languid circulation, as in the aged (their typical disease) and invalid and the intemperate; but it lays low vast numbers of the strong as well. The treatment has been revolutionized from the bottom, but still from one-fifth to one-fourth of all attacks are fatal. Thus far the most valuable novelties have been measures to prevent sudden heart failure.

(10) Malaria. Till a generation ago this was one of the obscurest diseases on our list; it still remains one of the worst

drawbacks to civilization, preventing general Caucasian settlement in the tropics. It was know to have an intimate connection with wet ground, marshes or the building up and sewering of new districts; to prevail chiefly in the fall, and be caught chiefly from dusk to dawn, and to be non-contagious. But nothing more was known till M. Charles Laveran, a French surgeon who had gone to Algeria specially to study the diseases, discovered the germs in the red blood-corpuscles of patients; not bacteria, but small protoplasmic bodies which begin as transparent rings inside the corpuscle, feed and enlarge on its coloring matter and form blackish grains from it, and on attaining a certain size divide and redivide in vast multitude, giving off a toxin which causes the acute spasm of fever, and apparently of chill also. Each variety of the fever is caused by a special form of the parasite. It was suggested by Dr. Patrick Manson, of London, that the communicating agent might be mosquitoes, also products of wet

ground and active after dusk; and an
army surgeon of India, Ross, found that
mosquitoes did transmit similar parasites
between birds—developing them in their
stomach cells into filary bodies, which
pass into the saliva and so through bites
into the bodies of others. It is now thoroughly established that this is the chief
means of transmission among human beings. The mosquito is not the common
culex of the Northern United States, but
chiefly the anopheles, which develops and
transfers the parasites as just described.
The crucial experiments are, that these
mosquitoes, allowed to bite malarial patients, and subsequently healthy persons
in non-malarious regions, infect the latter, and that in the deadly campagna
around Rome, two persons during the
worst season, from June 1 to September
1, 1900, lived entirely immune by simply
keeping behind tight netting after dusk,
while exposing themselves freely during
the daytime. The net result is, that
swamps and stagnant pools should be

drained, that . persons having malaria
should be thoroughly treated with
quinine so that they may not transmit
the disease if bitten by mosquitoes, and
that Europeans can live in the worst
districts by not being out after dusk and
by thoroughly wiring their houses.

(11) Venereal Diseases. These are in
one respect by far the worst of all we
have to mention, for they are the only
ones transmitted in full virulence to inno-
cent children, to fill their lives with suf-
ferring, and which involve equally inno-
cent wives in the misery and shame. In
the victim the infection does not stop with
the parts originally affected; and it has
not been seriously checked, from the nature of its causes making it impossible
for society to stamp out or much diminish
the actions which involve it. Physicians
and the public have each solemn duties
in this matter; the former, to act as apos-
tles of continence, especially with the
bachelors who pretend to believe that

their health needs the indulgence and will
not marry, and to use every effort to prevent the disease being carried to others;
the latter to let no scruples of delicacy
or affected ignorance stand in the way
of thorough public supervision. The op-
position to this is natural; women feel it
adding an unfair stigma to an already
shameful load or injustice; decent people
feel that legal recognition is legal pallia-
tion and defense; and there is the real
danger shown by experience, that if it is
once shielded by law, the weight of the
police force will be thrown on the side
of protecting instead of abating houses
of ill-fame, as with liquor saloons, but
with far more disastrous results. But any
risk is preferable to the present shocking
conditions, which make city brothels a
stream of contamination to what should
be the purest of homes.

(12) Puerperal Fever. Remembering
not merely the former fatality of this disease—terribly frequent in private prac-

tice, and in maternity institutions rising from five even to ten per cent—but the double bereavement it usually involves, the almost entire extermination of this disease is one of the grandest triumphs of modern medicine. Its contagiousness had long been suspected, when Oliver Wendell Holmes in 1843 published a full and clear statement of the facts leading to the belief; but for many years the profession generally scouted it—a wit and poet could be no authority in medical science. Others gradually took his view; but it was the Lister antispectic treatment which enabled it to be fully tested. Now the mortality is but about one-third of one per cent.

(13) Hydrophobia. This disease, though widely distributed among animals, is not very common among human beings in America, but excites a widespread horror from the multitude of pets, any one of whom may chance to be stricken and to communicate it; in Europe it is less

rare. The germ has not been isolated, but Pasteur ascertained its calculable effects on the nervous system and that certain inoculations could render healthy animals immune and neutralize a powerful dose of the virus. He founded an institution in Paris for its treatment, and the mortality among those bitten by certainly rabid animals was reduced to less than one-half of one per cent. In dogs, quarantine and muzzling are the only precautions.

(14) Leprosy. This is caused by a bacillus which probably enters the body through abrasions of the skin, and probably only from contact with another person; even so, it is but slightly contagious, contrary to the popular notion. It was discovered by Hansen in 1879, and since then an active and very hopeful investigation into prophylactic conditions has been carried on. Known to be old and widespread in Asia, it is not generally known that it came into San Francisco

with the Chinese, that the Norwegians have given it a considerable foothold in the Northwest, and that in Louisiana there is an endemic condition of it, and slightly in some other Southern States. It exists in New Brunswick likewise. Still more important for the United States is its great abundance in Hawaii and the Philippines. It can be readily kept in check by segregation and inspection.

Some other bacilli may be mentioned, of which the discovery has not as yet been followed by large results in prevention. The deadliest known is that of lockjaw or tetanus, discovered by Nicolaier in 1884; it enters by wounds, and in some tropic parts all lesions tend to develop tetanus as surely as other sections do gangrene.

Influenza, or "the grip," has one of the smallest bacilli known; it is spread by dried nasal discharges, and enters by the nasal tracts. Anthrax is a disease mainly of cattle and sheep. Its bacilli were the first micro-organisms of disease to be isolated, and can enter either by inhalation, infected food or abrasions.

Changes in Therapeutic Method.—It is only restating the same fact to say that new practice has followed on new theory, or, rather, new scientific knowledge of the nature of diseases. The only object of acquiring the knowledge was to embody it in practice. With the discovery of the zymotic principle in disease, traced finally to bacterial action, there could not be the same or like treatment as when the body was supposed to be possessed by conflicting "humors"; or when a fever was supposed to be an abnormal increase of vital fluids needing to be drained off; or when diseases were supposed to have no relation to any function of the body except the organs furnishing the dominant symptoms; or when one school supposed them waves of some sort, to be overborne by more powerful waves of the same class,

and another school refused to entertain
any theoretical suppositions at all, but
relied on the history of cases, printed or
traditional or experimental. But it may
be said that the greatest revolution in
the century, or at any rate the last half
of it, is in the position assigned to drugs.
At the outset the old faith in bleeding
still held great sway; Boerhaave himself
had made almost the whole art of medicine consist in its proper application, and
at the end of the 18th century Washing-
ton had been sacrificed to it. But by the
middle of the century it began to diminish. Both the homeopahic and the regular schools based their practice, and many
still base it, on the study and administration of drugs. They differed in the
size and strength of doses, from huge
boluses, or powders or draughts whose
efficacy was supposed to be in proportion
to their nauseousness, to small bland tri-
turations or dilutions; but not in the as-
sumption that in them lay the one efficient method of dealing with disease.

The advanced school of the present does not discard medicines; so far from it, it studies them with more care than ever, and values a few, well-tried and certain of quality and action, as highly as ever. It knows the mass of current medicines to be inert or worse, uncertain of action and applied to human functions of still more uncertain action; but it seeks to study thoroughly and apply scientifically the few real medicines or healing agents which must be used—quinine and digitalis, and opium, iron and mercury and iodide of potassium, etc.—instead of a swarm of dubious and varying materials. It is significant that some of the standbys are extremely old; iodine, as ashes of burnt sponge, was known in classic times, and ergot impressed its peculiar action on stockraisers' minds from very early ages; even Peruvian bark is nothing new. We have not as yet made as many additions to the stock of panaceas as we might. But chemistry has done vast services for us, and will probably do far more. Aside

from the discovery of new substances like
cocaine, it has given us the active prin-
ciples, of calculable strength and purity,
in place of crude drugs of varying strength
at best, and of varying purity and age;
and there is no reason why we may not
have new specifics as sure (and for as
important diseases) as quinine.

But the new school does not feel itself
under obligation to give any medicines
whatever, while a generation ago not only
could few physicians have held their practice unless they did, but few would have
thought it safe or scientific. Of course,
there are still many cases where the
patient or the patient's friends must be
humored by administering medicine or
alleged medicine where it is not really
needed, and indeed often where the buoy-
ancy of mind, which is the real curative
agent, can only be created by making him
wait hopefully for the expected action of
medicine; and some physicians still cannot unlearn their old training. But the

change is great. The modern treatment
of disease relies very greatly on the old
so-called "natural" methods, diet and exercise, bathing and massage—in other
words, giving the natural forces the full-
est scope by easy and thorough nutrition,
increased flow of blood, and removal of
obstructions to the excretory systems or
the circulation in the tissues. One nota-
ble example is typhoid fever. At the outset of the 19th century it was treated
with "remedies" of the extremest violence
—bleeding and blistering, vomiting and
purging, and the administration of anti-
mony and mercury and plenty of other
heroic remedies. Now the patient is
bathed and nursed and carefully tended,
but rarely given medicine. This is the
result partly of the remarkable experiments of the Paris and Vienna schools
into the action of drugs, which have
shaken the stoutest faiths, and partly of
the constant and reproachful object-les-
son of homeopathy. No regular physician
would ever admit that the homeopathic

preparations, "infinitesimals," could do any good as direct curative agents; and yet it was perfectly certain that homeopaths lost no more of their patients than others. There was but one conclusion to draw—that most drugs had no effect whatever on the diseases for which they were administered.

These "natural methods" have been indicated above; but some further analysis of the individual elements is worth while. It will be noted that this is not, as a hasty reader might assume, the discarding of all the results of civilization and a return to barbarism. That the natural methods are efficient is precisely because scientific knowledge and modern improvements in appliances, as well as the thousand civilized devices for comfort and cleanliness, unattainable even a generation ago, have raised them to the level of first-rate therapeutic agents.

Perhaps foremost in the rank is the trained nurse, who is not only a greater agent of philanthropy than many professed altruists, but sets free the physician from a load of care and anxiety. In place of ignorant and stubborn, usually conceited and often superstitious women, who pride themselves on defying all the doctor's commands, these intelligent and loyal women can be relied on to carry out all his injunctions, to watch carefully for indications of danger, and to furnish notes enabling him to view the progress and hourly changes of a critical case.

The importance of diet in therapy, and indeed in the preservation of health before the system becomes a subject for the physicians, has never been wholly lost sight of; but at no time has it been so thoroughly recognized, so firmly insisted on, raised to so high a place in therapeutic agencies. Too much food, improper or ill-prepared food, over-haste in eating, all have their part in the dyspepsia which is a byword among foreigners as the national malady, and though much lessened, is still most formidable. Over-eating, too, is largely responsible for the prevalent Bright's disease and degeneration of the arteries. Sweetmeats and the mixtures of the drug stores, ice-cream soda and artificial flavors, are other potent causes; especially among girls is the eating of candies between meals. The business man's five-minute meal at the lunch counter saves his business time often to the permanent ruin of his health. The question of alcoholic drinks is usually left to the forum of morals or politics; but it has a serious bearing on health, though not nearly so much as one or two generations ago. The introduction of light beers has not only lessened drunkenness, but organic diseases of the liver, stomach, heart and arteries.

Few influences on general health have been greater or more beneficial than the enormous multiplication of the means of cheap enjoyable outdoor exercise in

America within the past generation.
Owing to the climate, it is much harder
to keep up habits of steady exercise here
than in Europe, and unless there can be
sociability with it, most people will not
put themselves under the stress. We have
not been a people addicted to sport and
play, and formerly there were not sufficient means provided for us. Now tennis
and golf, and the bicycle and their kind
are improving the constitutions, especially the nervous condition, of vast numbers. Of course, there must be judgment
in these matters, and probably some
elderly people injure themselves by in-
dulging in severe athletic sports only fit
for young people with sounder tissues.

Massage need only be mentioned; its
aim is primarily to remove obstructions
to circulation. The normal blood should
be sufficient to establish normal bacterial
and other conditions, and massage gives
it the freest play. The essence of bathing, called when practiced scientifically

"hydrotherapy," is the same, save that its special function is to free the obstructed perspiratory system.

To these might be added a fourth, which in some sense is the most natural of all; for it has been practiced in ages more remote by many thousands of years than the suspicion of either of the others, and by savages almost at the bottom of the human scale; that is, some form of suggestion or hypnosis. The main difficulty of this sort of treatment is that so little has been done to make it utilizable in practice, or to provide any certain means of assuring a definite result. Another is, that as with all the forms of mental science, its vagueness, its mystery, the impossibility of regulating its manifestations, surround it with so hopeless an atmosphere of fraud and of that open-mouthed credulity which irresistibly invites fraud. Yet after all, the psychical method has always played an important, though largely unrecognized, part in therapeutics. It is from faith, which buoys up the spirits, sets the blood flowing more freely and the nerves playing their parts without disturbance, that a large part of all cures arises. Despondency, or lack of faith, will often sink the stoutest constitution almost to death's door; faith will enable a bread pill or a spoonful of clear water to do almost miracles of healing, when the best medicines have been given over in despair. The basis of the entire profession of medicine is faith in the doctor and his drugs and his methods. This is no new discovery; it was said by Galen that "he works the most cures in whom most have faith"; and the doctor-chemist-charlatan Paracelsus, who died of taking a universal panacea too poisonous even for his confidence, told his patients to have full faith and a strong imagination, and they would see the effects of it.

The subject of hypnotism, originally called mesmerism from its 18th century

describer and practicer, can only be
touched upon. Different practitioners have
had such varying results from its use as
to suggest that here, too, the personal
equation is very important. Braid of
Manchester, England, who first made a
scientific study and attempt at utilizing it,
was not successful; while an English surgeon in India, Esdraile, was highly successful, performing 268 operations on
patients, with all the effect of anaesthetics,
not then introduced. Its possibilities have
been greatly exaggerated, not so much
by the claims of the persons using it (except impostors) as by the eager credulity
of the public. It seems not so much to
create a new condition of sensitiveness to
suggestion, as to increase what normally
exists. In organic disease it is practically
useless. Its great service has been found
to be in various affections which may all
be classed as of the nervous system; hys-
teria, spasmodic functional complaints,
children's vicious habits, and the victims
of the drug and alcohol habits; occasion-

ally in childbirth and surgery, but it is
precarious and not free from serious dangers. It should no more be practiced
without witnesses present than dentists
give nitrous oxide, and the law should re-
strict its practice to special licensees or
physicians of a certain grade.

WILLIAM OSLER, M. D.,
Regius Professor of Medicine,
Oxford University.

CPSIA information can be obtained
at www.ICGtesting.com
Printed in the USA
BVOW06s1943150517
484199BV00016B/268/P